**DO NOT REMOVE
CARDS FROM POCKET**

Lyn St. James

by Mark Stewart

ACKNOWLEDGMENTS
The editors wish to thank Lyn St. James for her cooperation in preparing this book.
Thanks also to Integrated Sports International for their assistance.

PHOTO CREDITS
All photos courtesy Lyn St. James except the following:

AP/Wide World Photos, Inc. – 5 bottom right, 21, 29
Mark Stewart – 48

STAFF
Project Coordinator: John Sammis, Cronopio Publishing
Series Design Concept: The Sloan Group
Design and Electronic Page Makeup: Jaffe Enterprises, and
        Digital Communications Services, Inc.

LIBRARY OF CONGRESS CATALOGING-IN-PUBLICATION DATA
Stewart, Mark.
    Lyn St. James / by Mark Stewart.
        p. cm. – (Grolier all-pro biographies)
    Includes index.
    Summary: Presents the life and career of Evelyn St. James, whose love of mathematics and
sports led to a career as a professional race car driver
    ISBN 0-516-20175-1 (lib. binding) – 0-516-26023-5 (pbk.)
    1. St. James, Lyn—Juvenile literature. 2. Women automobile racing drivers—United States—
Biography—Juvenile literature. [1. St. James, Lyn. 2. Automobile racing drivers.
3. Women—Biography.]
I. Title. II. Series.
GV1032.S73S84 1996
796.7'2'092—dc20
    (B)   96-16771
                                                                                                            CIP
                                                                                                            AC

Grolier **ALL-PRO** Biographies™

Lyn St. James

by
Mark Stewart

CHILDREN'S PRESS®
A Division of Grolier Publishing
New York • London • Hong Kong • Sydney
Danbury, Connecticut

Contents

Who

Am I?

I have always loved going fast. But when I was growing up, women did not drive racing cars. For a while, I made the mistake of giving up on that dream. Then I thought, "Does a car know who's driving it? Of course not!" And that is when I started doing the thing I loved. My name is Lyn St. James, and this is my story . . . "

Lyn St. James

"I have always loved going fast. But when I was growing up, women did not drive racing cars."

Growing Up

Lyn St. James grew up in a home built among the mills and factories of Willoughby, Ohio. It was a strange place to live. There were only four houses in her entire neighborhood, and big trucks rumbled down the street at all hours of the day and night. There were no playgrounds, no parks, and no other children for her to play with.

Back then, she was called Evelyn, and her last name was not St. James, it was Cornwall. The Cornwalls lived near a factory that Evelyn's grandfather owned. The company built heating and air conditioning systems for homes and office buildings. Evelyn's father worked very hard, and there were many times when he did not come home until after she was asleep. Sometimes Evelyn would go to work with her father. She asked questions about all of the machines and tools he used, and she always wanted to know how the equipment he made actually worked.

Lyn takes some early steps with the help of her aunt Evy. Her mom stands behind them.

Because of where Evelyn lived, she could not do many of the things other kids did. There was no place to swim and it was too dangerous for her to ride a bike, so she never learned how to do either. Evelyn did show a talent for playing the piano. From the age of six, she played and practiced for hours each day and became a very good musician.

The Cornwalls moved into the center of Willoughby when Evelyn was 10 years old. She was very shy and did not always fit in well with the other kids on her street. Evelyn was not popular in school, either. "I was self-conscious all through grade school," she remembers. "I didn't

Lyn's first portrait

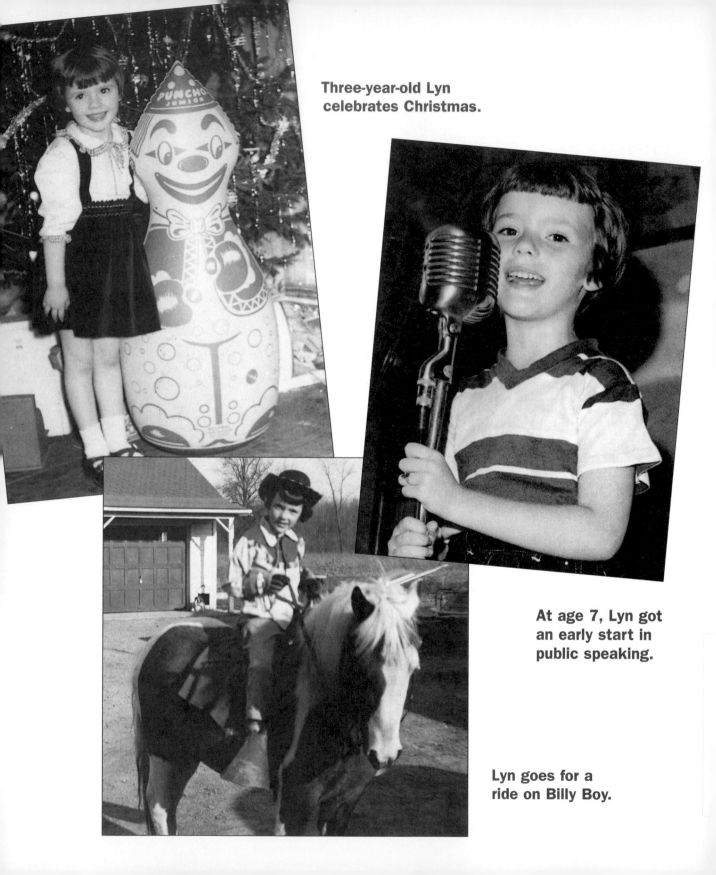

Three-year-old Lyn celebrates Christmas.

At age 7, Lyn got an early start in public speaking.

Lyn goes for a ride on Billy Boy.

have many friends, I never felt good about my looks, and I wasn't one of those girls who spent an hour and a half getting dressed in the morning. I felt that I was different. I think I just suffered from a lack of self-confidence."

After Evelyn turned 12, she made a big decision—without informing her parents. She felt that she would be happier going to a different kind of school, so she applied to the Andrews School for Girls just a few miles away. Only after she had been accepted did Evelyn tell her parents. They were very surprised that she would want to live away from home, but they knew there was no sense in arguing. When Evelyn made up her mind, that was that.

Evelyn blossomed at Andrews. Living with girls her own age on a 300-acre campus, she could be herself without worrying what boys thought of her. Evelyn started a friendship with a a girl named Karlene Pinkney, who encouraged her to participate in sports for the first time in her life. At first, Evelyn did not do well. She was not very coordinated, and she was not in good physical condition. Once, she passed out during basketball practice! But gradually, with encouragement from Karlene, Evelyn became quite good at games such as volleyball, tennis, and field hockey. Had she remained at her public school in Willoughby, she never would have discovered these sports. They were not offered to girls in public schools then.

Evelyn did as well in the classroom as she did on the playing field. Her favorite subject was math, especially the trickier subjects, such as algebra, geometry, and trigonometry. Her favorite teacher was Mr. Savitch, whose passion for music and the arts made him one of the most popular instructors at Andrews. The most difficult part of school for Evelyn was balancing her schoolwork, sports, and music. She also had to find time just to sit quietly and read.

"I was not great at communicating back then," she recalls. "And communication is a combination of reading, writing, and speaking. So I knew it was crucial to read as much as I could. I can't stress enough how important it is to learn to read. It gives you a way to express yourself, and enables you to understand and interpret things. Having command of the language lets you communicate with others, which I feel overshadows everything else you'll learn while you're in school."

When Evelyn was a junior, she moved back home while continuing to attend Andrews. It was then that her mother taught her how to drive the family car. The two Cornwall women would set out together on weekend adventures. After selecting an interesting place on the map, they would drive there on Saturday, and then return home on Sunday. Evelyn was allowed to do all of the driving, which was quite a thrill. Soon she became interested in things like what makes a car go and what makes it stop, so she took a part-time job at a local gas station. It was a grimy, smelly, sweaty job—and Evelyn adored every minute of it!

In the spring of 1963, 16-year-old Evelyn made a startling request. She wanted to attend the Indianapolis 500, the most famous auto race in the world. At first, her parents said no. But Evelyn begged for weeks, and finally her mother agreed to let her drive the six hours from Willoughby to Indianapolis on one condition: that they would go together! Once again, the Cornwall women hit the road. When Evelyn arrived at the Indianapolis Motor Speedway, she could not believe how exciting it was. The sights, the sounds, the smells—everything made her senses come alive. Evelyn wanted to explore "Gasoline Alley," where the racers and their crews prepared their cars, but she was told that girls were not allowed. The sting of this disappointment wore off quickly, however, when she got superstar A. J. Foyt's autograph. But Evelyn never forgot how unfair it was that women were not allowed near the cars.

The Road

When Evelyn Cornwall graduated from the Andrews School for Girls, she still was years away from beginning her racing career. She had, however, already been in her first race. Her love of automobiles had drawn her to a group of boys in Willoughby who sometimes entered their cars in drag races. One day, they decided to drive down to an event in Louisville, Kentucky. After one of her friends lost a race, she made a joke about it. Annoyed, he turned to her and said, "If you're so great, why don't you drive it?" To their astonishment, Evelyn climbed behind the wheel and won race after race. By the time she and her pals left the track, she was clutching the champion's trophy! When Evelyn told her mother about her triumph, her mother was appalled and ordered her daughter never to do it again. Any thought Evelyn had of racing cars for a living ended after that.

Evelyn's first stop after high school was the St. Louis

to Indy

Institute of Music, where she received her teacher's certificate. Later, she took an administrative job for an electronics company in Euclid, Ohio. There, she struck up a friendship with fellow employee John Carusso, who shared her love of racing. John and Evelyn were married in 1970, and they moved to Hallandale, Florida. There they started up an electronics company. At first, Evelyn was thrilled to own her own business. But when people called the office, they never wanted to talk to her—they wanted to talk to John. This made her angry. They were equal partners, yet everyone treated her as if she were John's secretary.

Some of the techniques Lyn learned playing the piano actually helped her in auto racing!

One day, her husband came up with a clever idea. Why not change her name? It sounded like a great idea. She decided her new first name would be Lyn—which is short for Evelyn. As for a second name, Lyn got her inspiration while watching "MacMillan and Wife," a popular show on NBC during the early 1970s. It starred the famous actor, Rock Hudson, and a young actress named Susan St. James. St. James . . . that had a nice sound to it, Lyn thought. From that night on, Evelyn Carusso was known as Lyn St. James!

There were other changes ahead for Lyn. After sinking every extra penny into their business for four years, Lyn and John took a few dollars and bought a Ford Pinto. They began racing it in regional events held by the Sports Car Club of America (SCCA). John did the driving, while Lyn acted as crew chief. Within a year, they were hooked on racing, and John bought a Corvette. Lyn went to driving school, received her SCCA competitor's license, and started racing the Pinto. Unfortunately, her career got off to a "flying start" during a race in Palm Beach, when she skidded off the track and plunged into a lake. It took two days to get the poor Pinto dried out! Lyn was not discouraged. In fact, she began to get excited when she realized that all of the math she had learned in high school helped her to understand how to push the car she was driving

Lyn won the 1976 Florida Regional SCCA Championship with a Cosworth Vega car.

to its limits. She knew this gave her an advantage over other drivers, who understood little about the science involved in gunning an automobile around a track. "I was able to use my math for something that I was excited and passionate about," she says. "For the first time, I really put my education to good use!"

Lyn had been driving for just two years when she won her first SCCA amateur championship in 1976. She then purchased a larger, more powerful car and won again in 1977. Not many women were driving competitively in the 1970s and few were as successful as Lyn. In 1978, she made it to the SCCA national championships. Meanwhile, John was enjoying some success of his own with the Corvette. He was competing on the International Motor Sports Association (IMSA) circuit and doing well. In 1977, he came in sixth at the annual 24-hour endurance race held at the Daytona Motor Speedway. It was the highest an American-made car had ever finished in the event.

Lyn should have been happy, but she was not. She wanted to be behind the wheel of the Corvette and told John so. When he let her enter the car in an SCCA race at Daytona, she won it. She continued driving the car that season until it was wrecked in a bad crash. Luckily, Lyn was unhurt and unshaken.

A wealthy businessman agreed to put up the money needed to race in the prestigious American Challenge Series. She rewarded his investment by finishing ninth for the year and winning the 1979 Top Female Driver award. That same year, Lyn had a chance to team with Janet Guthrie in a 12-hour endurance race at the Sebring Motor Speedway. In 1977, Janet had become the first

Lyn (right) with Janet Guthrie, the first woman to race in the Indianapolis 500

Lyn drove a GTO in the 1985 Sears IMSA race.

woman to qualify for the Indianapolis 500—something Lyn would one day do herself.

Lyn continued to win races and awards. In 1980, she received a factory contract from the Ford Motor Company, which meant that she got a car, a crew and all of her expenses paid—a huge step in a driver's career. In 1984, she joined the IMSA circuit and won Rookie of the Year honors. In 1985, she won her first race as a professional and got her first solo victory in a major race when she outdistanced the field at Watkins Glen. That summer, she also became the first woman to drive faster than 200 miles per hour. At the end of the season, Lyn was voted Norelco Cup Driver of the Year. For the first time, the Indy 500 seemed within her grasp.

The Story

From 1986 to 1991, Lyn St. James established herself as one of the finest and most versatile drivers in the world. She set numerous speed records and won prestigious races such as the 24 Hours of Daytona. All the while, however, Indy was on her mind.

Lyn's friends at the Women's Sports Foundation got the ball rolling. They collected $10,000 in private donations to fund her car, and then department store chain JC Penney agreed to pay for most of the remainder. The company was celebrating its 90th anniversary in 1992, so Lyn agreed to put the

Lyn gets ready to qualify for her first Indianapolis 500 in a car named "The Spirit of the American Woman."

Continues

For years, Lyn longed to compete in the world-famous Indy 500.

number 90 on her car. The Indianapolis 500 was just around the corner, and Lyn was ready to go.

When she got to the Indy qualifiers, however, her car was not. When Lyn took her first practice runs, the Lola-Cosworth engine felt like the one in her old Pinto. Only 33 drivers start the Indianapolis 500, and those 33 are the ones who record the fastest times in tests that take place during the week before the event. Lyn would not qualify with this car, and she knew it. She went to team owner Dick Simon and he agreed to let her try to qualify in the back-up vehicle of another driver, Phillipe Gache. Lyn hurtled around the track in this unfamiliar car, calling upon every ounce of skill and experience she could muster. When she flashed across the finish line, she had qualified easily.

Race day was cold and damp, but Lyn remembers it warmly—especially when the track announcer said, "Gentlemen . . . and lady . . . start your engines!" She knew early on that the 76th running of the Indy 500 would not be an easy race when pole-sitter Roberto Guerrero spun out on the warm-up lap. Lyn played it cool and just concentrated on avoiding the spin-outs and crashes that littered the track. Slowly but surely, she edged up toward the leaders, and finished the race in 11th place. It was a monumental achievement for a first-time driver, and she was the race's unanimous choice for Rookie of the Year. At the banquet following the race, Lyn received a standing ovation led by A. J. Foyt—the same driver who had scribbled his name on a piece of paper for her 28 years earlier!

Lyn reacts after qualifying for the 1992 Indy 500.

Timeline

1986: Receives *McCall's* Magazine Woman of the Year Award

1989: Sets 21 new national and international speed records at Talladega Speedway

1987: Wins IMSA 24 Hours of Daytona race with Bill Elliot

1991: Competes in the Off-Road Gold Coast 300

1994: Starts third consecutive Indy 500

1992: Wins Indy 500 Rookie of the Year award after finishing in 11th place

Making

Lyn drove in the 24 Hours of Le Mans in 1989.

Lyn kneels beside the car she drove in the 1989 24 Hours of Le Mans.

Tracks

In 1991, Lyn competed in an off-road race when she entered the Gold Coast 300.

In 1994, Lyn made headlines at Indy when she bumped international superstar Nigel Mansell to the third row by qualifying for the number six starting spot.

29

It's a fact of life in auto racing . . . you're going to have many more defeats than wins."

You need to get much more out of racing than a checkered flag or a trophy."

Lyn has been a member of the winning GTO team at the 24 Hours of Daytona race twice in her career.

I've experienced the lowest lows and highest highs in my life in racing."

In 1995, Lyn started her fourth consecutive Indy 500 to break Janet Guthrie's mark for women.

Lyn loves the competition of racing. "As long as I have the fire in my belly, I'll keep on racing."

Lyn, flanked by Emerson Fittipaldi (left) and Mario Andretti (right), acknowledges the fans during Driver's Day at the 1994 Indy 500.

Dealing

There are not many sports where you have to deal with the threat of death every time you play. But auto racing is one of them. Lyn St. James has seen other drivers die in crashes, and she has had a few close calls herself. In 1986, she was involved in a terrible wreck at Riverside International Raceway in California. Lyn was struck by several other drivers, sending her slamming into the wall. Her car then began to tumble, and when it finally came to a stop it burst into flames with Lyn strapped inside. She walked away with only two herniated disks, thanks to her protective racing suit and helmet. How does Lyn get back into a car after an experience like that?

At the Ford design center, Lyn helps evaluate new models for safety and performance.

With It

Protective head gear and constant tire changes help keep Lyn as safe as possible.

Motor racing is a calculated risk. But risk is like a muscle—you exercise it and learn to control it. And you have to keep pushing to make the muscle grow. It's not all guts and no brains. Walking away from my accident gave me more confidence in the car and my equipment."

The Grind

Lyn St. James has spent the past two decades proving she is one of the world's top drivers, male or female. But while many of the men in her sport have sponsors lined up to finance their racing teams, Lyn has had to work overtime for sponsorship dollars. To "get a ride," Lyn has had to agree to give speeches, make appearances, and grant interviews so that her sponsors get as much publicity as possible.

Lyn gives a speech on behalf of Ford Motor Company.

A publicity photo for Nike
Women's Fitness Apparel

I 've had to put up with a lot of stuff that others would never have tolerated. It's not easy being a woman racing driver, and sometimes it gets pretty lonely."

Lyn confers with former First Lady Barbara Bush.

Family

After nine years of marriage, Lyn St. James and John Carusso found that their racing careers were taking them in two very different directions, and they got divorced. Lyn remarried in 1993, to Roger Lessman, a real estate developer from Idaho. Roger has a daughter, Lindsay, from a previous marriage. They all live in Daytona Beach, Florida.

Right after their wedding, Roger and Lyn began working on a vehicle that they hope will establish a new land speed record in the fall of 1996. With Lyn behind the wheel, the Lessman Cruiser will take a crack at the current mark of 409 miles per hour.

Lyn snowmobiles with husband Roger Lessman and his daughter, Lindsay.

Matters

Say What?

Here's what racing people are saying about Lyn St. James:

"Do you see a woman competing with men in any other sport? No. But here she is competing with the best drivers in the world."

—*Dick Simon, team owner*

"Ability-wise, Lyn can do it."

—*Mark Raffauf, IMSA official*

"What she has done at the Speedway is incredible. But it's not just her racing record that's endeared her to the crowd. It's her charm, her rapport, and her class."

—*Bob Walters, Indy 500 official*

"Lyn never asked for respect—she went out and earned it on the track."

—*Emory Donaldson, IMSA driver*

"She doesn't abuse the machinery, she's extremely reliable, and she's one heck of a fine driver."

—*John McLaughlin, former crew chief*

"She gives fans what they don't get from other drivers. The others get too caught up in the racing. She doesn't let that get hold of her."

—*Johnny Capels, USAC official*

Career

Lyn St. James has few worlds left to conquer. She has competed successfully in almost every kind of race, driving almost every type of car. More importantly, Lyn has inspired a generation of young women to strive for greatness, regardless of the barriers they encounter. When she calls it quits, she will go down in history as the top female driver of all time. Until then, she will continue to look for the best cars . . . and beat the best drivers.

Lyn was the SCCA regional amateur champion in the Showroom Stock A Division in 1976 and '77.

Lyn races her JC Penney Indy car at Portland in 1993.

Lyn won the Watkins Glen IMSA GTO race in 1985 and earned GTO Driver of the Year honors.

Highlights

Lyn races for Sure on the SCAA pro racing tour.

Lyn was voted IMSA's Top Woman Driver in the Kelly Challenge Series each year from 1979 to 1981.

Lyn broke the women's speed record in 1988, driving 212.6 MPH in a Ford Thunderbird at Talladega.

Lyn won Indy 500 Rookie of the Year honors, finishing 11th overall in the 1992 race.

Reaching

Although Lyn St. James has one of the most demanding schedules in all of sports, she still finds time to get involved with several charities and women's organizations. From 1990 to 1993, Lyn St. James served as president of the Women's Sports Foundation, an organization founded by tennis legend Billie Jean King. The foundation's goal is to further the development of female athletes and to open up new resources for women to use in the advancement of their sporting careers.

"My time as president was a tremendous experience. It made me appreciate how far women have come in the world of sports . . . and how much farther we have to go."

Lyn signs posters for her fans in Mexico.

Out

Lyn is a guest at a
Girl Scout dinner.

Lyn works at a 1992
soap-box derby.

Lyn still likes to
give piano lessons.

In 1993, the Lyn St. James Foundation was created to provide instruction and training for aspiring race car drivers. Young people from all over the country attend her Driver Development Programs, which are held at the Indianapolis Motor Speedway and Charlotte Motor Speedway. The programs cover everything from driving to fitness to the business of racing—everything needed to prepare someone for the "road ahead."

"I always believed there was a void in the correct training of up-and-coming race car drivers. My focus was to create something that tapped into the missing elements. That's what my program is all about—taking people who have what it takes

to be professional race car drivers and giving them the knowledge, experience, and exposure to get them there. One doesn't need to have raced cars before. The key is having the right combination of raw talent, physical strength, mental toughness, drive, and determination."

Numbers

Name: Lyn St. James

Born: March 13, 1947

Height: 5' 6"

Weight: 130 lbs.

Lyn recorded her fastest Indy qualifying time in 1995. Sadly she was involved in a multivehicle collision that wiped out several cars in turn one of the race.

INDY 500 Record

Year	Main Car Sponsors	Qualifying Speed	Starting Position	Finish
1992	JC Penney/Agency Rent-A-Car	220.2	27	11
1993	JC Penney/Nike	218.0	21	25
1994	JC Penney/Reebok/Lee	224.2	6	19
1995	Whitlock Auto Supply	225.3	28	32
1996	Lifetime "Television for Women"	224.6	18	14

What If...

Just as it was once hard for me to imagine myself racing, it is hard for me now to think of myself *not* racing. Still, if something had prevented me from competing, I did have some options. The business courses I took in school came in very handy when I was a partner in my own electronics company, and my musical training could have led to a career as a teacher. My advice is to explore and be creative. Test your skills, test your interests and try different things. Then, figure out what it is that you enjoy doing. For me, that was racing. Find the thing you can really feel passionate about, and then follow your passion."

Glossary

EVALUATE to determine the worth or condition of something by careful study

HERNIATED DISK a painful condition in which the rounded, flat muscle tissues that support the lower back have been ruptured or torn apart

APPALL to be shocked or dismayed

ASPIRE to seek to accomplish a goal

CONSECUTIVE several events that follow one after another

POLE-SITTER the car with the fastest qualifying time that is given the lead position at the beginning of a race

RAPPORT an equal, harmonious relationship

VERSATILE having the ability to excel in many different areas; multi-talented

METRONOME a musician's instrument designed to mark exact time by a regularly repeated tick

MODES a particular form or arrangement of something; method; means

OFF-ROAD RACE a race in which the cars travel off the main roads, driving instead over the rough countryside

Index

About The Author

Mark Stewart grew up in New York City in the 1960s and 1970s—when the Mets, Jets, and Knicks all had championship teams. As a child, Mark read everything about sports he could lay his hands on. Today, he is one of the busiest sportswriters around. Since 1990, he has written close to 500 sports stories for kids, including profiles on more than 200 athletes, past and present. A graduate of Duke University, Mark served as senior editor of *Racquet*, a national tennis magazine, and was managing editor of *Super News*, a sporting goods industry newspaper. He is the author of every Grolier All-Pro Biography.